The Girlfriend Book

By Jo Ann Darby

Published by Warren Publishing, Inc.
Cornelius, NC
www.warrenpublishing.net

The opinions expressed in this book are solely the opinions of the author
and in no way constitute an official endorsement of any product or service.

ISBN 978-1-886057-77-7
Library of Congress Catalog Number : 2010921459
Manufactured in the United States of America

First Edition

17039 Kenton Drive, 101-B,
Cornelius, NC 28031

Dedication

The Girlfriend Book is dedicated to two of the most important "Girlfriends" in my life. The lovely young lady who motivates me each day to be an extraordinary woman, my daughter Alana and my mother Annette who is the backbone of my life. You both inspire me to be strong for myself and for the other women I am blessed to know.

I started *The Girlfriend Book* as a mother-to-daughter journal when Alana was four years old. Over the past seven years, I have gradually added to my collection of practical "every day" advice for my Alana culminating in the body of work I now share with my other "Girlfriends".

Among these extraordinary women are some of the most amazing "Girlfriends" any woman could ask for; my "mother-in-love" Faye Darby, my grandmothers Eloise Oliver, Louise Tuttle, and Susan Sharpe, my aunt "Tootie" Susan Coxe , Stephanie "Action" Edwards , Cindi "Scout" Van Wingerden, Shelley "Lully" Hartsell, Rena "Ney Ney" Taylor, Heather "Ace" Brown, Jennifer Cerick, Maria Lutzel, Beth Darby Hurley, Jody Darby, Katie "K Boo" Mulrooney, Bonnie "B Boo" Crittenden, Linda Bell, Stephanny "Fancy" deGorter, Jane Dupree and all of the clients of Lake Norman Skin Studio.

Thank you ALL for your words of encouragement, wisdom, and input to make the dream of this book become a reality.

I pray that women of all ages be inspired by the words I am honored to share with you.

I love you all dearly,
Jo Ann   "Jo Baby"

My Charity of Choice

DOUBLE HARVEST†
SOWING SEEDS OF LIFE

Double Harvest – Haiti
Tom Van Wingerden Memorial Fund
55 South Main Street
Oberlin, OH 44074
www.DoubleHarvest.org
440-714-1694

"Sow Seeds of Life"
in an impoverished situation

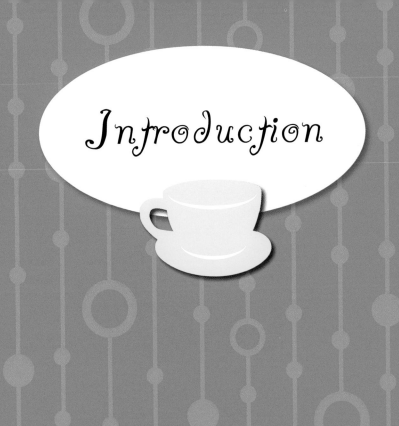

$\mathcal{W}$hen my daughter, Alana, was four years old we were out shopping - having fun, laughing and smiling big. I tried on a pair of shoes, one in brown, the other in black. I said "Sweetie, which one do you like best, the brown or black?" She, in her four-year-old voice, said "Dey are bowf fabulows Mommy!" I thought to myself, "They ARE both fabulous - buy both!" That was the day ***The Girlfriend Book*** was born:

"If you find a GREAT pair of shoes and they are available in black and brown, BUY BOTH! Don't think twice about it. You will regret not getting them and if you don't, chances are you'll go back and they will be gone!"

I started ***The Girlfriend Book*** for Alana's future reference. It contains all of my "golden nuggets" of wisdom, little shortcuts and insights about life so far. For years I have carried around a little notebook in my purse, slept with it by my bed, and taken it on trips. As a certified personal trainer and licensed medical esthetician, I've gleaned many insights from conversations with my clients during their treatments, as treatments often turn into therapy sessions. I have realized that women need to be encouraged and motivated about how special they truly are. Many of the tips in ***The Girlfriend Book*** are shared in hopes that they will encourage you to **live your life to the fullest.**

I owe much of the motivation to publish ***The Girlfriend Book*** to the clients of my medi-spa. They have seen me writing in my notebook over the years. They have all said, "You need to get that book published so you can share all of your goodies with other women!"

I have learned that a step of faith must contain action, so by publishing *The Girlfriend Book* I am simply following a passion from within. I hope you will find it to be like having an older sister who is willing to share her best kept secrets with you.

So, grab a cup of coffee or a glass a wine and curl up with heartfelt advice from a girlfriend!

Kind regards and full respect,
Jo Ann Darby

P.S. I am currently collecting tips, ideas and thoughts for the *The Girlfriend Book, Volume II*. It would be wonderful to have a collection of insights from women all over the world. If you will share your "nuggets" with me, I will include as many tips as possible, along with your name. If you want to submit a tip in honor of a special woman in your life, to preserve for future generations, I will include her name as well. Please send your comments to info@thegirlfriendbook.com , Facebook: The Girlfriend Book or visit www.thegirlfriendbook.com for information about starting your own TGFB Club.

This book is a compilation of opinions and is not meant as an endorsement of health care habits, products or procedures. Before using any health product or beginning any health program, be sure to check with your physician.

Beauty Secrets

> Be OKAY with your imperfections.
> NO ONE is perfect! Being OKAY with
> your imperfections makes you gorgeous!

- The curve of your smile keeps a lot of things straight!

- It takes about two weeks to get over a bad haircut.

- Wear mineral makeup; it allows the skin to breathe.

- Be preventative in the care of your health. Don't wait until you HAVE to do something about it. Prevention is easier than correction.

- The use of enzymes in skin care is very important. Enzymes are like Pac Man - they eat away at dead skin cells so that new, fresh ones can replace them. Enzymes force cell turn over. Dermalogica has an amazing daily micro-exfoliant and Glo-Theraputics has an incredible pumpkin enzyme as well. Pumpkin is one of the top enzymes you can use, so look for products that contain it.

- When your eye shadow/blush/powder starts to break apart, take your finger and smooth it down or it will keep breaking until there isn't any left.

- Use less makeup the older you become and use mineral makeup that doesn't settle into fine lines and wrinkles.

- To protect your hair color from damage caused by chorine, wet your hair in a shower or with a spray bottle before entering a pool.

- Place raw honey on a cut to help prevent scarring. – Marcela Karriker

Stand with one leg in front of the other to appear slimmer in photographs.
– *Annette Smith*

- Sit up tall and hold your arm slightly away from you while taking a picture to make your arm appear slimmer.

- When applying hair products, shield your face well. Many people break out on their face because of products such as hair spray or perfume. If you are breaking out around your neck it may be from the shampoo or conditioner that runs down your neck as your rinse. You may need to change products!

- A good source of Omega 3 is the brand sold by Coromega out of Carlsbad, CA. It's easy to take and it tastes like an orange creamsicle. Omega 3 is good for great skin and shiny hair.

- Want your hair to grow longer? Try prenatal vitamins - they contain folic acid and biotin. And be aware that hair grows faster during the summer months because of the heat.

- Extrinsic factors such as the sun, environment, smoking and drinking contribute to 70% of our aging. Contrary to popular belief, genetics play a small part. So, NO, just because your mother has beautiful skin doesn't mean you can go bake in the sun!

- Steps for a great looking self-tan: shower, exfoliate the body with a product that contains small beads and then shave. After showering, apply a creamy lotion and let it dry. Next, apply two thin layers of self tanner. Two thin layers are better than one thick one. I prefer spray tanners because they seem to go on more evenly. Neutrogena, Fake Bake and Sun Drench are great! Neutrogena takes a few hours to turn into a tan. Fake Bake and Sun Drench immediately spray on a tan. When you apply a spray, hold it out at arm's length, so you don't spray spots onto your skin.

- Foods that contain a high level of antioxidants are acacia berries, blueberries and pomegranates.

- Use the color wheel to select eye shadow colors that will make your eyes pop! For example, brown eyes look great with dark purple. And it is worth the time to make an appointment with a makeup artist for professional tips to maximize makeup for your skin and coloring.

- Clean and sanitize your makeup brushes regularly, especially if you are prone to breakouts. Jane Iredell has a great natural cleaner with grapefruit extracts that smells heavenly!

If you are taking a picture and the sun is in your eyes, close your eyes and tell the camera person to tell you as soon as they are about to take the picture. Then you can open your eyes and it won't look as if you are squinting.
    – *Ginger Wagoner*

- For a finishing touch after applying your makeup, spritz water into the air and walk into it. It will set your makeup.

- Whatever product you put on your face, neck and chest, put on the back of your hands too. Your hands are one place that shows age quickly.

- If your hair is oily and really needs to be washed, but you don't have time, simply sprinkle it with baby powder.

Before a performance, put Vaseline on your teeth to make them gleam.
– Marcela Karriker

- Dip the end of your toothbrush in baking soda for an inexpensive teeth whitener and stain lifter.

- Beautiful is an attitude - wear it!

- Change your pillowcase each day. Think about all the oils on your face that end up on your pillow each night. Silk absorbs oil, so think about a silk pillowcase if you battle acne.

- If you have worn braces and received a retainer afterwards, continue to wear the retainer periodically to keep your teeth from moving. Yes, even into adulthood.

- Wearing a very dark lipstick can make you look older. Wear a little pink on the lips for a more youthful look.

- Instead of frying yourself in the sun, use bronzer or a shimmer brick. Apply blush on your neck, below your ears, and on your neck and chest. It will look like you have a subtle tan.

- Take very good care of your teeth. Your teeth are the first thing people notice when they look at you, so a great smile goes a long way.

- Invest in a Sonic Toothbrush.

- Buy the Q-tip brand of cotton swabs - never the cheap kind.

- Apply concealer under your eyes with your ring finger. It has the least pressure of any of your fingers so you won't be pulling on the skin. The skin under your eyes is the thinnest skin you have. After you put concealer on, don't go back over it with foundation. It will look too heavy.

- When putting on perfume, spray it in front of you and walk into it. Then do it again. This layers the perfume and spreads it evenly.

- Walk with good posture. Walk with your head up and a smile on your face. Not cocky, just confident!

- Bring pictures to your hair dresser of the cut and/or color you want. Red to him or her may be different than red to you. Shoulder length to him or her might mean right above the shoulder and to you it might be right below the shoulder. Show them exactly what you want to avoid confusion and disappointment.

- Buy NICE makeup brushes - they are worth it and they last!
  Buy a travel set too to keep in your travel makeup bag.

- Be careful when plucking your eye brows, because it is so easy to pluck them too thin. It takes a long time to get them to fill back in. Plus, the older you become the growth slows down even more.

- Years of drinking out of a straw can lead to the development of lines around the mouth. Instead, try to slightly bite the straw and then sip.

- Remember, if you aren't making the lines (wrinkles), then you aren't creating the lines (wrinkles).

- Placing boiled, then cooled, green tea bags over your eyes reduces puffiness and dark circles. Another option to reduce puffiness is to rub ice cubes under your eyes.

- Curling your eyelashes makes a big difference.

- When applying mascara, turn the brush in the container instead of "pumping it". Pumping puts air into the makeup and causes it to dry out faster.

- To apply mascara, start at the base of your lashes and wiggle/zigzag up and out - this extends the lash. Let it dry and apply another coat for even thicker looking lashes. Hit the sides of the lashes really well for a dramatic effect.

- Hot water OPENS pores, cold water CLOSES pores. When you wash your hair, warm water is fine during the shampoo. Turn the water to cold while rinsing out the conditioner, even if it's just for a few seconds. You can then turn it back to warm once you've rinsed the conditioner out. All the good ingredients from the conditioner will stay in your hair as the pores close! The same thing applies to your face. After washing your face, rinse with cool water, to close the pores after cleaning them out. Shut them so they won't get clogged again. This also helps keep those pores tight and small!

- For shiny hair, wash with beer (for the yeast) and/or eggs (for the protein).

- If you have really dry hair, put a good conditioner on and then wrap your head with Press and Seal wrap, put a towel over it and sleep in it. Rinse in the morning for soft hair.

- Exfoliate your skin twice a week to encourage new cell turn over and to make your makeup go on great as well.

- When taking a picture, try sticking your head out like a turtle. This is a trick I learned from a professional pageant photographer, to obtain great head shots.

- Find a great esthetician and get a professional facial once a month to TAKE CARE OF YOUR SKIN! Start NOW!

- Perform self-spa treatments once a week. Set a day of the week (mine is on Sundays) to change polish, do a mask, pluck eyebrows, apply self tanner, etc.

- Brown Sugar is a great, inexpensive exfoliant. Brown sugar is made of little round beads which is perfect because it won't scratch the skin. Look at the ingredients of some exfoliation products and you'll find they contain crushed walnuts! Come on - this is your face, not your feet!

- Keep a pair of nice shears in your bathroom to gently snip the dead ends of your hair. This will encourage growth and will also keep your hair looking healthy.

- Use a toothpick to help guide false eye lashes into place. MAC's Duo is the best glue I have found. I use lashes from Wal-Mart instead of buying the expensive ones. After you use them and remove them, take tweezers to peel off the glue so you can possibly reuse them.

- Make a game plan for your skin care strategy! Timing is very important, so plan chemical peels for the fall, sunscreen methods for summer, etc.

- Do not pick at your scabs! Scabs are a protective covering for the skin, so it can repair and heal itself. If you pick at the scab it will just make the process longer because your body will have to produce another scab. Leave it alone and let it do its job.

- Putting toothpaste on a cold core or fever blister will take the sting out.

- Crest White Strips are very convenient and can be kept in your purse for a quick teeth whitener.

- A good night's sleep is a powerful beauty secret. Do your best to TURN OFF your mind, close your eyes and go to sleep. Remember, sleep is when the body is repairing, restoring and rebuilding itself.

- Brush your teeth within 20 minutes after drinking coffee, tea or dark colored sodas. After 20 minutes these can stain your teeth.

> Use peanut butter to get gum out of your hair.
> – *Linda Bell*

- For oily skin, use CLAY cleansers and masques. If you have oil build-up during the day, gently blot a tissue on your face to remove excess. Wiping will not only spread the oil, but ruin your makeup.

- For cellulite (orange peel looking) areas of the body don't buy expensive creams! Buy the store brand hemorrhoid CREAM (not ointment) and apply it like lotion over those areas. It creates a tightening effect. Great for days in shorts or swimsuits! Used coffee beans work too - it's the caffeine that does the trick. After you make coffee, take the coffee filter with the used beans and wrap it all in a paper towel so the wetness can still seep through. Rub on the areas you want to tighten.

- Salt water helps the healing process. When you get a breakout or cold sore, get in the ocean and it will clear up faster.

- Have a professional match your skin tone to makeup; otherwise you may end up throwing away the generic drugstore colors. The professional makeup really isn't much more expensive and department stores usually let you return makeup if you don't like it.

- Beat an egg white and then add oatmeal to it for an outstanding and inexpensive skin soothing and tightening mask. Leave it on until it becomes hard. It will get so tight that it will be hard to move your mouth! After this treatment, your skin will be less saggy and more toned, plus your pores will be tighter.

- Prevent wrinkles by sleeping on a proper pillow and using high quality skin care products. The quality of the product DOES make a difference.

- Wash your hands before you wash your face! Do not touch your face with unsanitary hands!

- The smaller the container, the less of that product you need to use. Don't waste money by using too much! The larger the container, the more you probably need to use. A good example is eye crèmes, a dab will do!

- If you have straightened or curled your hair and you need to take a shower, don't forget the old timey shower cap. They still work great!

- Taking a high dosage of ibuprofen can lead to thin blood, creating dark circles around your eyes. It shows up there because that is where skin is the thinnest. If you are having trouble with dark circles under your eyes, try Zyrtec Eye Drops. Also, allergies can make you appear to have dark circles under your eyes, so you may need to have an allergy test if the problem continues.

- GREAT PRODUCTS!
  Dermalogica
  Glo Theraputics & Mineral Makeup
  Redken Hair Products
  Aveda
  OPI Nail Polish
  Bobbi Brown Makeup
  MAC makeup
  Neutrogena Self Tanning Spray
  Ziploc Heavy Duty Freezer Bags
  Suave Body Wash
  Crest White Strips
  Gillette Disposal Razors
  Sonic Toothbrush
  Under Armor
  Burts' Bees
  Nivea Lotions
  Listerine Whitening Pre-Brush Rinse

Fitness & Nutrition

Nothing tastes as good as thinner feels.

- Consume antioxidants! A free radical is a molecule that isn't stable. It doesn't have an equal number of protons and electrons. Sun, drinking, smoking and other extrinsic factors cause electrons to disappear from our molecules. They then cause damage to other cells. This causes aging, and possibly cancer, so we must equip ourselves with antioxidants. Antioxidants calm free radicals by replacing missing electrons.

- Drink a lot of water! Sometimes people become very bloated and they won't drink water because they think it will make them look even bigger. What is happening is the body doesn't know when it is going to get water again, so it retains all it can. This is what creates a bloating effect.

- Your body will crave what you feed it. If you feed it sweets, it will crave sweets. If you feed it salads, it will crave salads.

- Put Vitamin C on your skin as a topical. Vitamin C is not produced by the body and is one of the most important vitamins for the skin. The skin is the body's largest organ, but it is the last to receive nutrients from the foods we eat.

- Calcium absorption takes place best at night. Take your calcium supplement right before you go to bed.

- It has been written that selenium may reduce the chance of breast cancer. Check with your physician on the safety before beginning any supplement!

- Krispy Kreme Doughnuts are worth gym time (especially the ones with the crème in the middle and chocolate on the top)!

- If you exercise first thing in the morning it will be off your mind and you will feel good all day.

- It's amazing what a new exercise outfit or new sneakers will do for your workout.

- Be accountable for the calories you consume! To lose weight you simply need to burn more calories than you take in!

- When you are pregnant, remember that your bones are softer, so when you exercise don't overdo it.

- Go to the gym for a cardio workout when one of your favorite TV shows is on. It makes the time fly by!

- It's better to eat little meals than huge ones. Each time you get hungry, eat a little something. Do not starve yourself. If you deprive yourself, you'll end up overeating. If you aren't hungry, don't eat! Eating out has become an "entertainment" for people these days. You can go out and enjoy being out, but eat a little of this, a little of that and have a good time.

- Cardiovascular exercise changes the SIZE of your body. Strength training changes the SHAPE of your body. If you have a "pear" shape body, and you do a lot of cardio, you will simply have a smaller, pear shaped body. You must do both cardio and strength training to achieve the results you want.

- When you go to the gym, have a plan for your workout. Cardio, upper body, lower body, a fitness class, etc. So many people go to the gym, walk in and look around not knowing what to do. Plan it out so you get results!

- Remember to work opposing muscle groups for optimal results. Also, work your larger muscles first.

- Chick-fil-A, in my opinion, is the greatest fast food restaurant EVER! They offer the best food, best service and great coupons.

- What is the best workout you can do? The one you WILL do! If you hate running, then you aren't going to keep it up. If you love to swim, then SWIM! If you love to walk, then WALK! You will stick with what you love to do.

- Learn your muscle groups. This will not only allow you to plan your workouts more effectively, but it will allow you to visualize the actual muscle you are working during the exercise. This will help you contract the muscle with greater intensity and your workouts will develop to their full potential.

- Drink ice water - it has a negative calorie effect. The body uses energy to heat up and digest the cold water. Since water doesn't have calories it ends up having a negative calorie effect – which is a positive for losing weight!

- Don't eat after a certain time (example: 7:30 pm) because if you go to bed on a full stomach your body is busy digesting what you just ate and not the fat you have stored.

- If you are trying to watch what you eat, prepare meals/snacks so they are ready to go when you are hungry. By not having them ready you end up eating whatever is available (usually junk food). Take a day that is not so busy (such as a Sunday afternoon) and prepare your meals/snacks for the week.

- Make exercise a HIGH priority in your life. Exercise is a natural anti-depressant. It releases endorphins that help keep you energized and happy.

- Use smaller plates, so you can easily control your portions.

- If you need an attitude adjustment, go exercise. MAKE yourself - you will be in a much better mood in an hour!

- If you are trying to watch what you eat and you have a party/dinner/event that you know will have tempting food, then eat healthy before you go. This way you don't go hungry and end up eating something you'll regret. The same tip works before going to the grocery store too. If you're hungry, you'll end up buying more.

- Drink a glass of warm water before going to bed to fight hunger pains. (Remember to try to go to bed on an empty stomach).

- Exercise for mental reasons, the physical results will come!

- When you exercise, let the mind go and allow the body to do the work.

- Do NOT diet. Just maintain a balance in eating. Don't deprive yourself of something. Instead eat a little bite, be done with it and move on. If you eat unhealthy foods today, then just tighten it up tomorrow! If you are getting ready to go on vacation and you want to enjoy being there, just tighten up what you eat before you go. ADJUST, don't deprive!

- Keep your colon clean. If you have trouble being "regular" (like many women do) try drinking magnesium citrate. Keeping your colon clean will help you obtain a flatter stomach.

- Doing hundreds of sit ups will not necessarily create a flat stomach. Watching what you eat will help you in this area. Cut back, balance and control your portions.

- The size of your closed fist is the portion size you need of protein.

- The size of your cupped hands is a snack portion.

- Muscle weighs more than fat, so remember when you are weight training: if you gain weight it's because you are building muscle. If you are more muscular, you will burn calories at a higher rate. Even if you are sitting still you will be burning calories at a higher rate than someone who isn't as muscular.

- Egg whites are an amazing source for a high protein, low calorie and low fat snack.

Drinking hot tea after a meal helps the digestive process by helping to keep everything moving along!
– Bonnie Crittenden

- After a day of strength training a particular muscle group, give it the day off. The resting of an exerted muscle is as important as the lifting itself. The muscle needs time to rebuild and repair. It's like the muscle is saying "Wow, she worked me hard! I am going to be bigger, better and stronger so the next time she calls on me I will be ready!"

- If you are seated for extended periods of time, such as being at work or traveling, do seated exercises. Squeeze your abs, flex your quadriceps and buttocks.

- When you want to accomplish an exercise goal (or any goal for that matter) obtain an accountability partner.

- The secret to great abs: when you are doing crunches, pretend there is a tennis ball between your chin and your chest. Push the small of your back into the floor or mat (if you can slide your hand between your back and the floor you are not pushing your naval toward your spine enough) and put your hands behind your head. If you can see your elbows out of the corners of your eyes then you are pulling with your neck – make sure your elbows are back! Finally, if you are doing all of these things and you still feel a pull on your neck, place your tongue on the roof of your mouth - this should release the pressure.

- When you want to improve your shape, clip pictures from a magazine, or of yourself when you looked your best, and post them on your bathroom mirror or inside your closet for privacy. This helps you visualize your goal. What you SEE, you become!

- The first stride is the longest when you start working out. It gets easier from there. You will get a mental high after a great session of cardio or resistance training. Getting to the gym is harder than the work out itself. Don't talk yourself out of going. Getting to the gym is the hardest part of exercise. JUST GO!

- Go by the way you FEEL and FIT into your clothes, not the scale. Remember muscle weighs more than fat, so as you strength train the scale may go up, but the inches go away. You don't want to become discouraged by weighing yourself.

- Need a little taste of chocolate? Have a mini Tootsie Roll. It will give you a taste of chocolate, without the fat intake.

- For a great cleanse after over indulging, use The Original Super Dieter's Tea by Laci Le Bean. I have found that the original is stronger than the flavored versions. Be aware that you have to time the cleanse just right for your body.

For example, eight hours after you drink it you will need to be in a place where you can have private bathroom time! More women have thanked me for this recommendation than I can count!

- Consider fasting one day a week. It clears not just the body, but also the mind and soul.

- The greener the lettuce or vegetable is, the higher the vitamin content. For example, choose a spinach leaf, as opposed to iceberg lettuce, as a salad choice.

- Check with you doctor before beginning any exercise routine.

Shopping & Fashion

True Strength. True Grace. True Beauty come from the Inside Out

- You can never have too many white shirts or black pants.

- Try things on. Sometimes you will be surprised how different clothes or shoes look once you try them on.

- If you try on a pair of shoes and they look great, but they are uncomfortable, don't bother buying them.

- When you are shopping, fill your cart with things you find interesting. Before you check out, do a review to see if there is anything you can do without, and if so, put it back. Holding on to it allows you to have time to think about it. There is nothing worse than to see the very thing you were looking at in some one else's shopping cart.

- To help keep your spirits up, buy yourself a little treat now and then, such as a new pair of shoes, new shirt, pair of earrings, etc.

> To stay classy: The shorter the dress, the lower the heels need to be. The longer the dress, the higher you can go with the heels.
> *—Annette Smith*

- Always spray your new suede shoes, purses and coats with a stain repellant to keep them looking new.

- If you are uncertain of whether or not to buy an item, leave the store and think about it. If you can't stop thinking about it, go back and get it. If you forget about it, you don't need it. If you are still unsure, place it on hold, sleep on it and decide the next morning.

If you want to wear a great outfit, but don't have the money to go out and buy a new outfit, just buy new accessories. New accessories change the look of an outfit and give you the feeling you are wearing something completely different.

— Katie Mulrooney

- If all of your clothes are hanging in the same direction, it is much easier to see what you want to wear. To do this, hang all of your items of clothing on their hangers with the hooks facing in the same direction.

- Use the same style hangers for your clothes so they hang evenly at the same level. Organize your closet into groups: Short sleeves, long sleeves, jeans, skirts, dresses. Then organize by color within those groups.

- The best deals and clearance sales are in January and July.

- When you are making sales calls from home, get dressed up. Being dressed up makes you feel more professional, which will come across in your pitch.

- Walk with confidence, looking forward, not down at your toes!

- If you find a GREAT pair of shoes and they are available in black and brown, BUY BOTH! Don't think twice about it. You will regret not getting them and if you don't, chances are you'll go back and they will be gone!

- Men to fall in love with: TJ Maxx, Marshall & Ross.

- When you wear denim, don't overdo it by wearing too much. For example, don't wear jeans and a jean jacket at the same time. If you are wearing jeans, wear a colored jacket and vice versa.

- If you are wearing big earrings, don't wear a big necklace, big belt or a top with a lot of decoration on it. That's just too much "bling bling!"

- Shoes can change the whole look of an outfit. My mom always said, "There is nothing a new pair of shoes can't fix." She's right!

- You can never have too many pairs of black shoes or too many LBD's (little black dresses).

- When you are at stores like TJ Maxx, Marshalls or Ross, looking through the racks to find good items, make sure you FEEL the fabrics. Learn the FEEL of a good quality fabric and you can get amazing deals.

If something doesn't look right, (you are under or over dressed for a party or your hair is a mess) act like it's supposed to be that way. Play it off! People will think, "Well, I guess she meant for it to be like that." The more you act self-conscious about it, the more it will draw attention.
- Susan "Tootie" Coxe

- Get rid of anything that you don't really love in your closet. This way you'll love everything you wear!

- Lucky Jeans and Miss Me can make your butt look great! They are worth the extra money.

To make the neck of your turtleneck shirt stay up, pin it in the back. This will help it stay in place, so it doesn't keep falling down.
- *Shelley Hartsell*

- Ask for light starch instead of heavy starch at the dry cleaner. Heavy starch breaks down the fabric faster, so by requesting light starch you will lengthen the life of your clothes.

- To make a bandana: fold the fabric diagonally, from corner to corner, and then roll it up from the point.

- NEVER EVER buy an acrylic sweater, not even if the percentage of acrylic is low. Acrylic fabric looks cheap.

- Make a list before you go to the store. If you don't, you will end up buying things you don't really need or even want!

- Hear me and hear me clearly: A COACH purse is worth EVERY CENT you have to pay for it!

- Buy or order bathing suits for the summer in the first quarter of the year, January to March. The newest styles are coming out then and they disappear fast. The good ones always go first! I love Venus swimwear because you can mix and match styles and sizes for the tops and bottoms.

- Buff your leather shoes with a product foam buffer. It makes a big difference in your outfit when your shoes look maintained.

- When you have to wear high heels, and it's going to be a long day, slip a pair of comfortable shoes in your bag so you can switch to them if you get an opportunity. You can put your heels back on when you need them. It ruins the effect when you are trying to look like a million bucks, in smoking hot shoes, but you are limping from blisters!

- Save the tags off new clothes for awhile just in case something goes wrong and you need to return them. I once purchased a dress, but didn't wear it for three weeks. As soon as I put it on the zipper broke. I was able to return it only because I had saved the tag!

> For an extra lift remember to tighten your bra straps!
> – *Stacy Possert*

- Don't dry your bras in the dryer - it tears them apart. They will last longer and keep their shape better if you line dry them.

- When you are doing a "practice run" for special occasions, take a picture of yourself in the outfit. This helps you perform a "self check" by showing you if you have a hair out of place, too much or too little makeup, if an outfit adjustment needs to be made, if earrings are the right pick, etc.

- Take pictures of the outfits you like so you can remember how you put it all together.

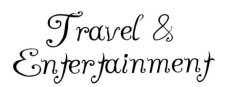

Travel &
Entertainment

> You are a little of each person you meet and a part of the environment you are exposed to.

- For football games, concerts and live events, it is really worth it to upgrade your seats. It will change the whole experience, so don't be a cheapie here.

- After you go on a trip, restock your travel bag with the things that are low such as shampoo, Q-tips, lotions, etc. This way when it's time to go on a trip again, you are stocked with all your toiletries.

- Find a place to pick up dinner on your way home from being on vacation. It's too hard to come home from a trip and unload, do laundry, go through the mail, care for the animals and then try to cook and clean up after a meal.

- Give yourself a day after you come home from vacation to get caught up on bills, laundry, and errands before going back to school or work. Friday to Friday vacations allow you to have a full weekend at your destination and then have another weekend to return to normal.

Before hosting a party get everything ready and then leave yourself an hour or more before guests arrive to compose yourself, relax, take a bath and get ready. A grumpy hostess is worse than bad food! Tell everyone not to disturb you during this time. Get someone to help you so you can do this, even if it's on a trade.

– Cindi Van Wingerden

- Always take diamond stud earrings and hoop earrings on every trip.

- Buy doubles of your cosmetics, so you can have a set for home and a "to go" set. This way you aren't going back and forth trying to find where you put this or that. This is extremely helpful it you travel frequently.

Have someone who is good at taking pictures take charge of documenting your evening. Remember, pictures are all you have left after the evening is over!
– *Cindi VanWingerden*

- Go on vacation every quarter, even if it's a mini-vacation. Getting away from your normal environment clears your head. And going different places gives you a different perspective, which broadens how you think, which changes who you are.

- Go on a BIG trip at least once a year. It gives you something to look forward to, work for and stay in shape for.

- When you travel, carry a lot of smaller bills, such as ones and fives, for tipping. This way you don't have to over tip because all you have are large bills.

- When you go on a trip, pack things that could leak in a Ziploc freezer bag. Take extra bags with you for the return trip in case something does, in fact, leak.

- Try to experience the Ritz Carlton at least once in your life. They have the most impeccable customer service. You can learn a lot by going there and watching and listening to the staff. That kind of courtesy should be enjoyed and duplicated by more people and businesses.

- When you are going on a cruise, the fastest way to get to the boat from the airport is to take a cab. Don't take the cruise ship transportation - you will have to wait for the entire bus to fill up before they leave. It's totally worth it to grab a taxi.

- When you are traveling, instead of trying to capture pictures of the places, monuments, and events that you are seeing, just buy the postcards instead. They are usually better than the ones you can capture and it's a better use of your time. Pictures are much more interesting to look at with people in them, so make sure you ask someone to take your picture instead of just trying to capture the monument or view by itself.

  When you travel, place a piece of paper with your contact information on it, inside of your luggage. If your luggage becomes lost or the information tag falls off someone can still find you.
  - Annette Smith

- Place a small change of clothes in your carry-on bag in the event your checked luggage becomes lost.

- Create a charm bracelet with unique pieces from all the places where you have traveled. Every place you go, get a charm. Make sure to have the charms soldered on since sometimes the loops that come with them don't work well. Soldering each charm guarantees they won't fall off.

- When staying at a hotel, pull the bed spread down. They do not change these after every customer. Yuck!

- When packing your clothes for a trip, try rolling them up. This not only saves space, but it helps prevent wrinkles.

- Take a little medicine bag with you on trips filled with things you might need, such as Excedrin, Motrin, Neosporin, stool softener, Gas-x, Sudafed, etc. You may not need them, but if you do, you will be thrilled you brought them.

- When you go on vacation and eat at a great restaurant, stay at a nice hotel or meet an interesting person, journal about it.

- Capture your 'special moments' in a journal so you can look back on them later in life.

- Make several photocopies of your passport. Take a copy with you on international trips and leave one with someone you can reach back at home.

- When you write in your journal, use lots of descriptions to tell about the small things, about what you saw, things people said and how you felt instead of just writing a list of things you did.

- Before an event, check your camera battery. So many times, I've pulled out my camera to use it and the battery is dead.

- When you take a dessert to a party or as a treat to someone, carve their initials or name into the top. This is also fun if they just had a baby, to carve the baby's initials in the top.

- When you go out for the night, make an agreement with a friend to do "chick checks" throughout the evening (lipstick needs replacing, hair needs to be fixed, false eyelash is coming off, etc).

- When you pay with a credit card at a restaurant they usually bring you three receipts. One as an itemized bill and two that you can tip, total, and sign. Sign one and TEAR up the other one. Your card has already been processed through the machine, so someone can just sign the duplicate and give themselves a bigger tip!

- You are asking for a hangover if you go to bed with a "buzz." Let it wear off first, drink a large glass of water and take ibuprofen before you go to sleep.

If you are going out with friends, have a 5 minute "P& D" warning, so everyone knows to pee and/or get a drink of water. Also, make sure everyone has their MMILK- Mobile, Money, ID, Lipstick & Keys.

- Cindi VanWingerden

Friendship

> Choose to spend your time with people who inspire, motivate, encourage and uplift you. You ARE who you associate with, so be cautious of the company you keep.

- Keep a list in your phone or planner of people who are special to you and what they like so when it's time to buy them a present you can refer to it. (Example: Nana likes teddy bears, Mimi likes dogs and Dad likes cuff links)

- Keep pictures of friends who send you picture Christmas cards (I scan them). It's fun to look back over the years to see how people have changed.

Sharing a bottle of wine with someone can change things.
– Hunter Edwards

- A true friend loves you during the good and bad times. They will answer honestly if you ask them if they have misbehaved and they won't judge you if you have.

- Don't let a small disagreement ruin a great friendship. If it's a TRUE friendship it will work out.

It is the QUALITY not the QUANTITY of the friends you have that is important.
– Beth Darby Hurley

- Don't smother people! Give them space! One friend can't be everything for you. You have been given different friends for different reasons. You may go to one friend for one thing and another friend for something totally different.

51

Place positive quotes, Bible verses, favorite sayings, etc. on a bulletin board, pretty vase or special area in your home. When a friend visits, suggest that they take one with them as a special treat to uplift their spirit. It could be just what they needed to hear and it's also a nice way to celebrate friendship!

– April Monroe

• Be quick to listen to your friends, but slow to speak.

– Traci Shiles

• Each person you meet has a "best seller book" inside of them. Just listen - they are a masterpiece!

- Rose Monroe

• It takes two to tango! Look at all the angles! There are always two sides to a story.

• Surprise someone you love with a bagel and coffee at their desk for when they get to work.

• Do something special and unexpected for a friend.

• When you are out with a friend, buy her a little treat to remember the day.

• Host a "big girl" tea party or slumber party! Have facials, massages, makeovers and play games!

• If your girlfriend asks your opinion about something, like what she's wearing or about buying something, tell her the TRUTH. A true friend tells you like it is. Remember you can tell someone you don't care for something in a nice way.

• To have good friends you must BE a good friend.

Home Economics

> When your house is clean,
> your mind is at rest.
> - Faye Darby

- When you make sweet tea, remember that it will get sweeter overnight, so be careful not to make it with too much sugar.

- Lasagna (really any pasta) is better the next day. Cook it, refrigerate it, reheat it and then eat it!

- Iron clothes before putting them away. When you're ready to wear them, they'll be ready too!

Light all the candles in your home and then blow them out. Never have a "new" wick showing.
- *Southern Lady Rule*

- Take sugar cookies out of the oven as SOON as the bottoms turn slightly brown - even if the cookie doesn't look thoroughly cooked. Pull the cookie sheet out of the oven and allow the cookies to cool right on the cookie sheet, THEN remove the cookies with a spatula. This makes the cookies nice and crisp!

- Clean sheets help you sleep well. Nothing is better than slipping into a nice, comfy bed with clean, crisp sheets. So, change your sheets frequently. I change mine almost every other day - it's worth the extra laundry.

- Parkay's Spray Butter helps you get the butter flavor without using so much butter and fat.

- Buy albacore tuna in WATER not oil.

Don't dry your jeans; they will shrink up. After you pull your jeans out of the washing machine, hang them up to dry. Once they are fully dry, place them in the dryer with a fabric softener sheet for a few minutes. If you want to tighten your jeans, wash them in hot water and then place them in the dryer.
- Rena Taylor

- Buy Mott's or White House Applesauce - the store brand usually isn't as good.

- Super Wal-Mart has a good selection of meat.

- In the winter when you have the heat on, place a pot of water on the stove to add moisture to the air.

- Instead of washing clothes that really don't need it, hang them up and spray them with a fabric refresher, like Febreeze, and then allow them to dry. It's a good way to keep your clothes looking new and it cuts down on your laundry.

- Take your clothes out of the dryer while they are hot, so they don't wrinkle and you have less to iron.

- Purchase nice sheets, at least 350 thread count, made of Pima or Egyptian cotton.

- There are lots of uses for dryer sheets other than just as a fabric softener. They can also eliminate odors in a variety of places:
  - Gym bags
  - Inside shoes in your closet
  - Under the seat of your car
  - In your dresser drawers
  - In the center of a roll of toilet paper in your bathroom
  - Under the trash bag in your trash can

- When you buy bread, pull a loaf from the back of the shelf. It will usually be fresher. Look at the color of the tag on the bread, as it reflects the day of the week it was placed there. The beginning letter of the color means it was placed earlier that week. For example:
  -Blue-placed in the earlier part of the week
  -Green
  -Red
  -Yellow
  -White-placed later in the week

Wrap rubber bands around your brush handles, so they are accessible when you need them.

- Alana Darby

- I love Styrofoam cups and Tervis Tumblers because they don't sweat! Wash them, keep them, and reuse them because they can't be recycled and will end up sitting in a land fill.

- Take the time to wipe down the kitchen or bathroom sink after you use them. It makes the whole room look cleaner. So does a made-up bed.

- I would give up cable TV before I would give up my cleaning ladies! A clean home will give you a clear mind and it's hard to have an entirely clean house if you do it yourself. It's worth the money to come home to a totally clean house. If you are a stay at home mom, you have all the more reason to have a cleaning lady. You need the break because you are NEVER off work!

- Velveeta cheese makes the best grilled cheeses sandwiches.
  Use a cast iron skillet to make the bread a little crispy.

- Mirrors make a room appear much larger.

- Use a paper towel to open the doors and touch the handles in public restrooms.

- If you spill something on your clothes, use a dab of club soda to remove it.

- Using a cast iron skillet adds iron into your diet.

If you are in need of a lint roller and one is not available, use a damp washcloth.
    – Annette Smith

- After a candle loses its wick there is still good smelling wax left. To get your money's worth out of the candle: Place the candle in a glass jar, put the jar on the coffee pot burner and then turn the burner on. It will melt the wax and smell as good as if the candle were still burning.

- Store brand canned veggies are as good as the name brand ones, so save your money.

- In December, host a cookie or dessert exchange. It's a great way to have a variety of holiday treats, but you only have to do the work of baking one item. Especially if you have guests coming for the holidays, this is a nice way to be able to offer different treats to your holiday guests.

- Never leave the house with appliances still running, such as the dryer.

- Lowes Home Improvement Center has a great selection on lighting. It looks like you've gone to a high end specialty lighting store.

- For all those single socks that lose their mate in the laundry: Place a basket on a shelf in your laundry room and every so often match them up. It's amazing how they show up over time.

- Before relighting a candle, snip off the black burnt part of the wick. This will stop the candle from burning black smoke and create a still flame.

- Make sure when you make a bed that the sheets underneath are pulled tight. This makes the comforter look better.

- To load a bag of icing: Put the coupler down in the bag first, and THEN cut off the bottom. If you don't, you can cut the bag tip too big. Also, don't fill the bag full of icing or it will just come up out the top. Fill 3/4 full, then twist and tie. As you use it, keep it twisted so the icing doesn't come out of the top.

- For good creamy icing, let the butter sit out at room temperature (no-no to the microwave here!) then mix with confectioners' sugar, vanilla and a splash of milk. Blend with a good mixer (I prefer Kitchen Aid) and let it run until the icing is really creamy!

- When making homemade cookies, make the dough and icing and bake the cookies on one day then decorate the cookies the next day. If you try to do it all in one day you will be tired by the time you are ready to decorate and the cookies won't be as cute.

- Always use French's Onion in recipes, not the store brand (Sheppard's pie, around chicken dipped in egg, green bean casserole, etc).

- Put a tablespoon of vinegar in your laundry. It is a cheap laundry booster.

- Keep Oxiclean stocked. It is one of the best products out there! (Works great as a carpet cleaner too.)

- When you have a piece of clothing that is heavily dyed, such as a tie dye shirt, soak it in salt before you wash it. This sets the color. Then wash the item separately.

- Viva Paper Towels are the softest.

- Learn the names of ingredients in products, so you can tell exactly what you are getting. Remember, the first ingredient listed is the one with the highest content in the product. Ingredients are listed in descending order based on amount in the product.

- Burn candles every day to create a soothing home environment.

- Use your "good stuff"; don't save it for a special occasion. Make every day a special occasion!

- For good cinnamon toast: evenly spread the butter, sprinkle the sugar on and then hold cinnamon way up high and tap, tap, tap the jar so it goes on lightly. Toast for three minutes. (I am famous in my kids' world for my cinnamon toast.)

- Step on cereal, soda and snack boxes before placing them in the trash can. They will take up less room and you won't have to take the trash out as often.

When loading the dishwasher; place all the forks in one slot, the spoons in one slot, knives and so on. When the cycle is finished simply grab all the spoons at once, then the forks, etc. and place in the drawer. This makes putting dishes away faster. – *Lei Timberlake*

- When you have a lot of laundry to do, place all the towels together as a load in between hard loads such as whites. This gives you a nice break between loads with easy folding. Do the same with sheets and jeans - a load of just sheets, just jeans or just towels.

- Tide detergent seems to keep colors in clothes bright. Tide also has a great pen to take with you that works well on spills. Gain smells great!

- When you have flowers in a vase and the stems start to look bad, but the flowers are still ok, put green food coloring in the water. Then change the water every few days, since the flowers may smell good, but the water stinks.

- To cook sausage, put water in the pan and then fry.

- Don't buy rubbery cucumbers - the small pickled ones are the best. Smell the cantaloupes and buy the ones that smell the most fragrant. Buy the smaller squash - the big ones aren't as good. Knock on a watermelon and buy the one that sounds hollow.

- Iron your t-shirts (yes, I know this sounds crazy) to make them look like they are brand new. This also works for worn looking clothes and fabrics that bead up.

- When you are planting flowers, buy them one day and unload them from your car and then plant them the next day (Lowe's Home Improvement has the largest variety of flowers). Or buy them a little bit at a time and plant them. If you try to do it all in one day, you feel like your back is broken!

- When you are planting flowers, break up the roots so the energy of the plant spreads. This will allow the flower to grow bigger.

- When you are injured use RICE: Rest, Ice, Compression, Elevation

- Even the smallest gift looks amazing with a great wrapping job! To make your present look professionally wrapped, after you have the box wrapped, run your fingers along all the edges from corner to corner. It gives a sharp crisp appearance. Top with a fabulous bow!

- When putting your towels away after laundering them, rotate towels from top to bottom so you don't use the same towels over and over and they all have equal wear and tear.

- When shopping in the dairy section remember to look at the dates of cheese, yogurt, sour cream and milk. Reaching for one in the back may give you a later expiration date. They move the ones to the front that they need to sell earlier.

> When screwing or unscrewing something try to remember: Lefty Loosy, Righty Tighty.
> *– Paul Taylor*

- It is worth the extra money to buy the brand name marshmallows, such as Kraft Jet Puffed.

- Goo Gone is great for removing price tags, especially for something you are giving as a gift. Keep it on hand.

- Rinse your bathing suit out as soon as you come back from the pool, lake or ocean to prevent the color from fading.

> White rice helps a stomach ache.
> *– Faye Darby*

- When you have bananas and/or strawberries that are close to going bad, peel the banana and cut the tops off the strawberries and place in a Ziploc freezer bag to use later in smoothies.

• When you are cooking a big meal, place a paper bag beside you to discard items. This saves you from having to visit the trash can over and over.

– *Beth Darby Hurley*

• Bake bread in your home before a dinner party or event. It gives the home an inviting smell and feel. This is also a great idea when you are trying to sell your home. Bake bread right before you have a showing to tap into the buyers' emotions!

• Use applesauce instead of oil in your baking to reduce fat.

Cooking Substitutions by Sylvia Morris:

Baking Ingredients:
Baking Powder (1 tsp) = 1/4 tsp baking soda plus 1/2 tsp cream of tartar

Semisweet chocolate (6 oz of chips, bits or square) =
9 tablespoons unsweetened cocoa plus 7 tablespoons sugar plus
3 tablespoons shortening

Cake flour (1 cup) = 1 cup all purpose flour minus two tablespoons

Self-Rising flour (1 cup) = 1 cup flour plus 1/4 tsp baking powder
& pinch of salt

All-Purpose flour (1 cup) = 1 cup flour plus 2 tablespoons cake flour

Whole-wheat flour (1 cup) = 2 tablespoons wheat germ plus
1 cup of white flour

Vegetable oil in cakes = apple sauce, measure for measure

Sugars/Sweeteners:
Brown sugar (1/2 cup) = 1/2 cup white sugar plus two tablespoons of molasses

Light brown sugar (1 cup) = 1/2 cup dark brown sugar and 1/2 cup granulated
sugar; or 1 cup granulated sugar and 1 tablespoon of molasses

Confectioners' sugar (1 cup) = 1 cup sugar plus one tablespoon cornstarch
processed in food processor, fitted with metal blade

Superfine sugar = Granulated sugar mixed in the food processor, fitted with the
metal blade, until it is powdery. Then measure powder.

White granulated sugar (1 cup) = 1 cup firm-packed brown sugar,
2 cups confectioners' sugar, sifted OR 3/4 cup honey OR 1 1/4 cups molasses
(reduce other liquid in recipe by 1/4 cup or add 1/4 cup additional flour if no
other liquid is called for)

Honey (1 cup) = 1 1/4 cups sugar plus 1/4 cup water

Molasses = 3/4 cup brown or white sugar plus 1/4 cup water

Dairy Products:

Buttermilk (1 cup) = 1 tablespoon vinegar or lemon juice plus enough milk to equal 1 cup. Allow to stand 5 minutes. OR 1 cup milk plus 1 3/4 tablespoons cream of tartar plus 1 1/2 teaspoons lemon juice. Allow to stand 5 minutes.

Dairy sour cream (1 cup) = 1 cup plain yogurt
OR 1 cup buttermilk
OR 1 cup evaporated milk plus 1 tablespoon vinegar
OR 1 cup cottage cheese pureed with 2 tablespoons milk and
1 tablespoon lemon juice
OR Heavy cream (1 cup, not for whipping)
OR 3/4 cup milk plus 1/3 cup melted butter or margarine
Or 3/4 cup milk plus 1/4 cup melted shortening or butter
Or 2/3 cup evaporated milk

Half-and-half (1 cup) = 7/8 cup milk plus 3 tablespoons melted margarine or butter
Or 1/2 cup heavy cream plus 1/2 cup milk
Or 1/2 cup evaporated milk plus 1/2 cup milk

Yogurt (1 cup) = 1 cup buttermilk

Butter (1 cup) = 1 cup margarine OR 7/8 cup vegetable shortening
OR 7/8 cup corn oil

Cream Cheese = Equal amount cottage cheese blended with cream
to correct consistency

Crème fraiche = Equal amount of sour cream

1 cup finely crushed crumbs require:
24 round (Ritz) crackers
28 saltine crackers
14 graham cracker squares
22 vanilla wafers
3 cups uncrushed cornflakes

Be with someone who "fills" your cup as much as you "fill" theirs.

- No matter how long you are together, ALWAYS stay boyfriend and girlfriend. Make time each week for a date night.

- Before marrying someone, it's a good idea to date them for at least a year, through every season, but not more than two years. You can get used to having your cake and eating it too!

Give respect to a man and he will give you the moon!
– Marcela Karriker

- Love people according to THEIR love language! SPEAK THEIR LANGUAGE: Acts of Service, Quality Time, Physical Touch, Words of Affirmation or Gifts. This is based on the book *The 5 Love Languages* by Gary Chapman, a great book to READ!

- Even when you become a wife, still keep the girlfriend personality! Stay fun!

- Learn the game of football. It is SO exciting and guys love it when they take a girl on a date and she actually understands the game.

- Marry a person you love talking to and who really listens to you. As you get older, their conversational skills are as important as any other skill.

- Pick a mate who will go to a "click flick" with you.

- If you marry someone for their money, it will be the hardest money you ever earn.

- Family is EVERYTHING. Treat them well.

- Little things that get on your nerves about someone will REALLY get on your nerves years later, so be careful who you decide to spend the rest of your life with.

Write a journal together.
   - Beth Darby Hurley

- When you say "I Love You" to someone, mean it or don't say it.

- Be engaged for at least six months before you get married so you can really enjoy the time building up to your wedding.

- Be able to agree to disagree.

- When you are planning your wedding, stay firm in the way YOU want it to go. It is YOUR wedding.

- Love deeply and passionately. You may get hurt, but it's the only way to live life fully.

- Treat those you love the very BEST. It's crazy that we are short and snippy with our friends and family members, but on our best behavior with people we don't care about deeply, such as co-workers.

- Have family pictures made at least once every year.

- Be with someone who loves you so much that they would be willing to run after you.

- To find a good man: Watch how he treats his mother, sister or sister-like figure in his life and how he treats animals.

- Women speak an average of 50,000 words a day. Men speak an average of 25,000 words a day. Don't take it personally if your man comes home and doesn't feel like talking. He has probably maxed out his quota!

When you are upset, try to talk to your kids, spouse, mother, father, sister, brother, girlfriend, or boyfriend, as though there is a stranger listening. This will help you speak kindly even while getting your point across.
– Cindi VanWingerden

- Ordinary things can be extraordinary when shared with the right person!

- When a man gives you a gift, accept it graciously. Don't comment on how much it may have cost or say the money shouldn't have been spent. Accept it with a smile and be thankful that he WANTS to spend lavishly on YOU!

- Usually when the "bedroom" is good the relationship is happy and healthy.

- When you are dating a guy and he reacts in a LARGE way to a small situation, event or comment – RUN from the relationship, don't just walk. This is a clear sign of someone with a high temper and it is a true warning sign to you. If a small problem equals a big response then it equals big trouble down the road!

Communicate, communicate, communicate!!! Things left unsaid are like sweeping dirt under a rug. The bigger the pile gets, the harder it is to clean up.

- Beth Darby Hurley

- Set long and short term goals together. This helps you stay on the same page in life.

- Men need to completely understand that when they are good to a woman she reciprocates!

Wedding Tips from Lindsey Wallace Van Wingerden:

- Planning a wedding is a special time when you learn more and more about each other as a couple and you bond closer together during the experience. And not only do you learn more about your future spouse, but you also learn about your friends and family, who will be there for you, who won't and who is true to you. It is a real eye opener!

- Don't stress about every little wedding detail. Will the person sitting at the table next to you really know that they have a different ribbon on their menu??

- Document every wedding moment you can! You will look back on them and be glad you did.

- Don't put things off to the last few weeks. Your wedding will be here before you know it!

- Enjoy your engagement time - it will be gone in a flash!

- Candles can change the whole ambiance of a room and are cheaper than expensive lighting!

- You have to be happy with yourself before you can be happy with anyone else.

- Your circle of friends will change when you are in high school and college, when you get married and when you have kids. Some friends will stay and others will go, but it all happens for a great reason. Be ok with making new friends!

> Find what you love to do and then find a way to make money doing it.

- Try to go away to a big college. Leave home, spread your wings and fly.

- Join a sorority - later in life you will be glad you did!

- Helping others be successful leads you to be successful.

- For important business meetings don't carry in a briefcase/computer case and a large purse. Consolidate your items because carrying too much does not look professional.

- Set BIG goals and then break them down into smaller goals that you can obtain one at a time.

- Sometimes you have to do what you don't want to do, to be able to do the things you want to do. Be willing to do what others won't do, to have what others don't have.

Keep an up-to-date resume.
– Beth Darby Hurley

Keep a three ring binder with all of your certificates of achievement, classes taken, awards received, a copy of your diploma, samples of your work, etc. It's a great way to keep a running portfolio of your success.

– Heather Brown

- Be careful about going into business with family or friends. Things might get "sticky" and it's difficult to manage relationships mixed with money.

Learn how to manage upward.
— Beth Darby Hurley

- When you are really good at something don't do it for free.

- Work out trades with people in other professions. For example, I would trade an hour facial for an hour massage.

Find a way to be visible in all parts of your company, not just the department you work in.
— Beth Darby Hurley

- When doing business with someone, learn personal things about them. Do they own an animal they cherish, what sports team do they love, what is their favorite candy, what hobbies do they enjoy? Bring them little treats regarding those particulars. They will greatly appreciate your thoughtfulness. Doing good business is about building good relationships.

Never take credit for something you didn't do.
— Beth Darby Hurley

- WRITE down your goals, dreams, desires and visions. Then visualize yourself obtaining them. There is something powerful about writing them down on paper.

- Learn to think with a long term vision, not just a here and now mentality. See the bigger picture!

- If you want to teach your children how to be successful, you must SHOW them what it looks like. Success can mean many things, not just monetary achievements.

- Know how to relate to ALL types of people. Know how to talk to a biker and to a banker! Be able to have a conversation with a variety of people.

  Don't participate in company gossip.
  – *Beth Darby Hurley*

- Figure out ultimately what you want, where you want to be and work backwards from the goals to obtain them.

- You can increase your brainwave activity by sucking on a peppermint candy! Try it the next time you have to take a test – it really does help you focus.

  Be slow to hire but quick to fire.
  - *Beth Darby Hurley*

- When you get to be in upper management, a business owner, leader of a group, or a committee chairperson make sure to surround yourself with good people who are good at what they do and who care about you. And make sure to give them the credit and praise when they deserve it.

  Always have your business card on you.
  – *Beth Darby Hurley*

Happiness

> Live with passion!
> Whatever makes your heart pound,
> whatever you think about most
> - THAT'S your passion!

- Be wary of a person whose actions and words don't coincide. Also, be wary of people who SAY "you can trust me." You shouldn't have to tell someone to trust you; you should show them they can trust you with your actions.

- Everyone is dealt a "hand of cards" in life. How you play those cards is totally up to you! Don't let past experiences cripple you. LEARN and GROW from your experiences. Make YOURSELF better; don't rely on someone else to do it. That won't happen. Don't blame someone else for what they did to you. At some point you have to put that behind you.

- Wake up every day and think to yourself: "What can I do that's fun today?" "How can I make myself a better person than I was yesterday?" & "What can I do for someone else today?"

- There is a purpose for your life! Find it and live it!

- Like YOU! Love YOU! When you like yourself, when you love yourself, others are attracted to you because you carry something different. The difference is you are happy with yourself. You are happy in your own skin.

- When you take care of yourself, when you take TIME for yourself, you are a better spouse, mother, sister and friend. DO NOT FEEL GUILTY for giving to yourself! For Example: Putting your kids in child care while you work out.

- It is a true gift to be able to place yourself in other people's shoes. Place yourself in what they are going through and how they see things. You will be more compassionate.

- Somewhere, someone has it worse than you! Happiness is SIMPLY A CHOICE!

- Your weakness ends up being a tool for you to learn about yourself. It allows you to help guide others who are going through similar situations. Helping others, teaching others and guiding others through their struggles helps wash away not only their challenges, but yours as well. You both end up being stronger individuals.

- Learn to sing! Sing A LOT! Sing out loud!

- You cannot change anyone. They have to want to change themselves. Don't worry about them, just worry about YOU!

- When you are driving down the road jamming to your favorite song, singing along with your head bobbing and you pull up to a stop light with someone in a car beside you - keep SINGING! Who cares what they think! In fact, they'll be thinking "Look at her, so full of life. I wish I had the confidence to do that!" They will look at you and SMILE!

- You are responsible for your own happiness! You are NOT responsible for anyone else's happiness!

- Give people more than they expect and do it CHEERFULLY!

- Try not to go to bed mad. You won't sleep well.

- When making a big decision (job, financial, love) sleep on it. It's amazing how this clears your thoughts. Make a rule with yourself that you will sleep on it and don't compromise.

Even if you make mistakes in life it's NEVER too late to change and make something BIG happen!
- Dan Tuttle

- It's a funny thing - the less you have, the more content you are. The more you have, the more you have to worry about. Live simply.

- Remember, my dear, great love, great reward, and great achievement involve great risk! But GO for it!

- If you lose, don't lose the lesson.

- The R's to remember: Respect for yourself, Respect for other people, Responsibility for YOUR actions.

- Always have something to look forward to and something to be excited about to keep you from getting "down in the dumps."

- No one is going to make it "happen" for you -YOU have to do that for yourself.

- Remember how to PLAY! Be a kid again!

- When you want to do something badly enough, you will find a way to make it happen!

Buy yourself fresh cut flowers every once in awhile. Don't wait for someone else to do it - do it for yourself and it will make you smile!
– Katie Mulrooney

- If you want a change, you must do something differently! You cannot keep doing the same thing and expect a different result. If you are driving north on a highway and you need to be driving south, at some point YOU MUST TURN AROUND or you will just continue to go north. Be willing to change!

- There is something GREAT to notice about everyone. When you notice it, tell them!

- Watch the old *I Love Lucy* episodes if you want a good laugh! Think about the issues they addressed in 1952 and how many of them are the same issues we deal with today! Another plus is you can actually watch them with your children without the worry.

- Wake up in the morning and set your intentions for the day. If you KNOW what they are, you will feel more successful at the end of the day.

- You never know how one small thing you say to someone might make a HUGE impact on their life.

- Don't rely on anyone to make you happy - that is YOUR JOB!!!

- Expect GREAT things to happen and they will!

- Write down your thoughts, concerns and prayers. It's amazing to look back and see how you've truly been blessed. If you don't write it down, you end up forgetting about it.

> Don't EVER settle for less than you deserve!
> – *Cindi VanWingerden*

- Make a "bucket list" of the things you want to do in the near future.

- Remember to take good care of yourself, so you can take good care of others.

- Take a few minutes each day to reflect, journal and have a quiet time, even if you have to get up early to do it.

- Always, always listen to your inner voice or inner spirit. It will NEVER lead you down the wrong path. Don't ignore it!

- Take a chance on yourself!

- People cannot debate HOW YOU FEEL. If you are in an argument and you say you FEEL a certain way, you can never be wrong.

- Everyone should own a convertible at some point in life! (Love my MINI Cooper!)

- Discover Michael Buble's music.

- Smile when answering the phone, people can hear your smile.

- Find YOURSELF! Be happy with yourself!

- Give a smile away - it's free! When you are passing someone you don't know – smile. You have no idea what they are going through and your simple, passing smile may give them the little extra boost they need.

- Live everyday to its fullest! You don't know what your future holds.

- Wake up every day expecting something really great to happen. E-X-P-E-C-T!

- Changing the way you think changes the way you feel, which changes the way you act, which changes how you live your life. Changing the way you think changes your life.

- Keep your life exciting!

- Keep your life simple as well!

- If you allow yourself some time, it's amazing how your thoughts and desires change.

- Your mistakes will help mold you.

- BE TRUE TO YOURSELF! You can tell people what you think in a nice way!

- Things don't have to be perfect, to be perfect! News flash - they will NEVER be perfect so enjoy your life today!

- Never give up on your dreams - they have been placed in your heart for a reason. Believe in who you are and the purpose you have been given.

- When you find yourself in a "waiting period" of life, think of it as time to develop as a person. Just like an egg placed in an incubator - if you pull it out before it's totally developed it won't survive. But if you wait the full waiting period you end up with a cute little chick!

- Remember, one wrong move can make a change in your life forever. Think through decisions you need to make carefully.

- One person you meet can change the complete course of your life.

- TRY HARD then TRY HARDER!

- Don't say "yes" to things you really don't want to do. Say "no thank you!"
  If you don't say "no" you will end up being unhappy and not much fun anyway.

- Stop worrying about things and situations that are completely out of your control.

- If you don't know WHO you are anymore, if you have forgotten WHO you are,
  if you have misplaced YOU (this happens a lot to women who have young children)
  you will always feel like you don't belong anywhere. Go find yourself and
  LOVE her, she is a GOOD GIRL!

Life can only
be understood
backwards, but
must be lived
forwards.
– *Terri Mc Connell*

- Life seems the best when it is SIMPLE.

- Be careful of the timing you use to discuss situations with
  someone. Timing is as important as the issue at hand.

- Getting rid of the old makes room for the new. Let go of the
  past so you can move forward!

- Be in the NOW, be in the moment, be where you are.
  This is how you live IN JOY!

- It's all about what you tell yourself. See the blessings in EVERYTHING,
  good and bad.

- Don't take life so seriously or you will be miserable.

- Focus on the positive. If you look for the negative you will certainly find it.

- Action is required in a step of faith!

- When you are down or depressed go do something for someone else. It will get your mind off of yourself! Sometimes depression is caused by dwelling on what we think we need or on what we don't have. By giving to someone else you don't have the time to focus on negative things. When you GIVE of yourself to others you create happiness.

- After reading something, go back at a later date and read again. It's amazing how the very same words can mean something different to you in another "season" of your life.

- Be GENIUINE! People can FEEL it!

- When you are speaking to a child, bend down to their eye level and look them in the eyes. This makes them feel that you are interested in what they have to say or you really mean what you are saying to them.

- Stop being so hard on yourself!

- The grass is NOT greener on the other side. It's just a different shade of green!

- Be joyful without NEED or REASON.

In life, whether it is what your parents give you or what you give your kids, remember it may not always be equal, but overall it's usually pretty fair.
 – *Cindi VanWingerden*

- Doing something you are afraid of cures you at your core.

- Instead of shutting off - turn ON!

- Be a new YOU every day!

- If you are "in the dumps" and feeling depressed, go to a store that sells greeting cards and read the cards in the funny section. You will be laughing out loud before you know it!

- If not NOW, when? If not YOU, then who?

- Realize that life is a journey. It will always be a journey, so learn to enjoy it instead of simply enduring it. Experience everything life has to offer!

Don't keep things you don't use. Get rid of clutter!

- If you have a big day planned, decide the night before what you are going to wear and get it all ready - ironed, accessories picked out, shoes chosen, etc. The same goes for anything else you may need - books, papers, etc. Have them ready to go by the door so you start your day organized. You don't want to be running around in chaos!

- Take the time to back up all your pictures and documents on an external hard drive and place it in a fire proof box or safe-deposit box.

- Make a list of things you need to accomplish, in order of importance, and do the important things first!

- Organize your errands in a loop, to save time and gas.

- When you buy something new, give something old away.

Keep plastic Ziploc bags (Large/XL/XXL) in the trunk of your car. They're great for when you pick up the kids from practice and don't want grassy/stinky cleats, helmets, football pads and muddy shoes in your car.

– Sondra Monroe

- Keep a small notepad in your purse or by your bed so you can write down your thoughts and your to-do's. You can also have a place in your phone to store notes. Write them down or you WILL forget.

- Before you begin your day organize your tasks by places to go, things to accomplish and emails/calls to make. Place a square by places to go, a circle by things to do and a triangle by calls/emails.

Don't let papers pass through your hands more than one time. Do something with them immediately. That way you won't waste time on the same things and you will eliminate clutter.
– Beth Darby Hurley from Kathie White

- Save all of your receipts in an accordion file. It saves a lot of time when you want to return something to be able to find the receipt quickly.

- Buy a scanner and scan all of your papers. It gets rid of clutter and forces you to organize your files.

- Keep baby wipes in the car even if you don't have a child. It is like having a wash cloth anytime you need to wipe sticky hands, wipe up a spill or wipe your mouth.

- Always write down the name, number, and extension of the person you are speaking with. Especially if there ends up being a problem, you will have proof of who you spoke with and can refer back to your notes.

- If you can't get it all done, perhaps you are trying to do too much. Life is short - slow down!

- Keep a pad and pencil by your bedside table so you can write down thoughts, ideas and to do's to get them off your mind before going to sleep.

- Download, organize or label your pictures once each week. If you don't keep up with the task, it will become overwhelming. Pictures are ALL you have left of times past, so take lots, but keep them under control by organizing them often.

- Don't throw away boxes from important purchases. It's helpful if you need to return the item, but also helps with phone numbers and website information regarding the product.

> Follow through! Totally complete your task! For example, don't place items on your staircase to take up later. Take them up right away and put them where they belong.
>
> – *Kristi Papst*

- Write down important information from the cards you carry in your wallet. If your wallet gets stolen or lost, you will have the numbers to cancel them quickly. You could also photocopy everything and place it in a lock box.

- Label cords with the items they go with or you will end up with a bunch of cords that you have no idea what they are for. Place extra cords and instruction manuals in Ziploc bags and write on the outside with a Sharpie what they contain. (IPod accessories, blackberry accessories, camera accessories, etc.)

> Make your bed each morning. It is much more inviting to come home to a neat bedroom after a busy and hectic day.
>
> – *Karen Radley*

- Place papers, pictures, programs and souvenirs that you aren't sure what to do with in a designated drawer. At the end of each year, place them in a large Ziploc bag. Label them by the year and place them away until you are ready to do something with them.

Words of Wisdom

> ## When in doubt, do nothing!
> ### -Bob Darby

- Instead of pepper spray, keep a large can of wasp spray on hand. It shoots further and stronger.

- Be aware of your surroundings and who might be watching you.

- When you light a match, run it under water before throwing it in the trash can. Even a slight spark could start a fire in the trash can. When you hear a little sizzle you will know for sure it is out.

- When you are carrying a cup of hot coffee or tea, just walk normally and you will be less likely to spill it. The slower you walk, the more likely you will be to spill it on you.

- If you are having surgery, remember that anesthesia can make you constipated so you might want to think about taking a stool softener.

The best dreams happen when you are awake!
- Marcela Karriker

Dance like EVERYBODY is watching - instead of "like nobody is watching." Otherwise, what's the point?
- Marcela Karriker

If you don't A-S-K you don't G-E-T!
– Denise Bledsoe

- If you have a hard time going to sleep and you want natural help, take a melatonin supplement, a warm bath and spray lavender on your pillow.

- If someone tries to take your purse, throw it away from you so that they will run after it. Then run in the opposite direction. NOTHING is more important than your safety.

- If you are in a situation and need to utilize self defense, remember that your elbow is one of the strongest parts of your body. USE IT!

- Don't take the stairwell in a building if you are alone.

- When walking to your car alone in a parking lot, walk fast and boldly, while looking around you with your keys in your hand. Hold the key to your car between your index and middle finger, so it could be used as a weapon if necessary.

- Never walk to your car and then start digging through your purse to find the keys. That is a perfect opportunity for a robber to be aggressive.

- When you are getting in your car alone, glance in the back seat to make sure no one is back there! Also, don't sit there digging through your purse or checking off your to do list without locking the doors and looking around you.

- If someone gets in your car and tells you to drive off, it is better to wreck the car, on the side they are on, than to go where they tell you. You might get hurt, but it would probably be better than what they plan to do to you.

- Learn how to do things CORRECTLY the first time so you don't learn the wrong way and have to teach yourself over again. It's hard to learn it over. For example, if you learn the wrong form for tennis or golf, you will have to relearn the entire swing.

- It's a lot easier to keep yourself out of trouble than to get yourself out of trouble. Be careful not to slip and fall into a "hole" that, if you had just paid more attention, you wouldn't be in, in the first place.

- When you are buying electronic devices, remember that the more gadgets it has, the higher the risk of something going wrong with one of them.

- When reading, gathering information or listening to a speaker, take from it what works or applies to you and leave the rest. It is okay not to agree with everything they say, but you may learn a new point of view. Be open to new ideas, but be firm in what you believe in.

Before you go to bed, hand over all your problems to God. He will be up all night anyway!
- *Kim Lawrence Curry*

You can do much more with your imagination than with knowledge because you must have the ability to visualize first!
– *Marcela Karriker*

Remember, you can never count your blessings too many times!
– *Crystal Sossoman*

If you are sad, go to a third world country.
– *Marcela Karriker*

- Invest in a good digital camera. The small ones are great to keep in your purse, but for important events it truly makes a difference to have a good camera.

If you are torn between eating pizza or practicing yoga - do both! Eat your pizza standing on your head.
— *Marcela Karriker*

Be grateful for your blessings and tell yourself, "THIS or SOMETHING BETTER". Believe that where you are and all you have is from your Source. — *Debbie Lee*

Wake up each day and align your heart with what is good and right for you. Respond to what the day holds, knowing it is for your greater good.
— *Traci Shiles*

- Don't: Believe all you hear, Spend all you have or Sleep all you want.

- The truth can set you free, but that doesn't mean it won't be painful!

- When you are going through struggles and adversity, focus on getting through that hour, that day, that week - one baby step at a time. Focusing on one moment at a time will get you through the situation. Even when you feel like a slug that someone poured salt on, believe that you WILL make it! I tell myself that I am like an oak tree, planted firmly by God, on purpose. I do not wavier in the wind; I WON'T wavier in the storm. My base and foundation only grow stronger, thicker and deeper with each trial!

Always keep a positive attitude and a smile on your face no matter what you are dealing with. It not only uplifts your spirit, but those around you as well!
— *Cathy Mamone*

Say to yourself, "Of course I can do anything. I am a Woman!"
– Marcela Karriker

Crying makes it feel worse. Breathe deeply and laugh instead!
– Marcela Karriker

Sometimes you learn more by keeping your mouth CLOSED!
– Denise Bledsoe

Trials give you an opportunity to experience God's ability to sustain you.
– Allen Darby

Finances & Spending

> The most important things in life
> can't be deposited into a bank account.

- Live below your means, get debt free and stay that way! Make a plan to obtain this and then work the plan.

- Don't buy anything that you can't pay for now!

- Keep your credit score high! Always pay off your credit cards at the end of each month. If you cannot do this then you are living above your means and it will come back and bite you in the butt.

> If you have to wonder if you can afford it, you can't.
> – *Bob Darby*

- Don't buy something unless you completely love it. You will end up getting rid of it and wasting your money.

- Sometimes there is nothing you can buy that feels better than the money in your wallet.

- It's better to buy less of the good stuff - furniture, clothes, etc. - than to buy a lot of the cheap stuff.

- Think about buying a slightly used car, so that when you drive it off the lot you don't immediately lose money. Finding someone who needs to get out of a lease can be a win-win for everyone.

Pay with cash! When you have to fork over the "Benjamins" you think twice about what you are buying. When you pay with credit cards you end up buying more and spending more than you would if you were paying with cash. — *David Gretzy*

- If you are bartering or negotiating and you aren't embarrassed by your offer, then you aren't going low enough.

- Try not to rent. Find a roommate who will rent from you which helps YOU pay your mortgage. When you sell the property, you will get money back instead of having nothing to show at the end of a rental lease.

- Make sure you love what you are buying MORE than the money you have worked hard to earn.

- It's not about how much money you make, but about how much money you KEEP!

Choose to spend more money on classic items than on trendy ones. Buy timeless pieces of furniture and classic styles of clothing. — *Stephanie Edwards*

- Do not get behind in paying your taxes. It is very difficult to catch up!

- Live off of 70% of your income. Put aside 10% for tithe, save 10%, allocate 10% for taxes and then live off the rest. Adjust your lifestyle to fit this model.

- Each quarter, take a good look at your expenses and shave off anything unnecessary. You'll be surprised to find things that have crept into your budget and increased your spending without your awareness.

- When you get a gut feeling that you need to reduce your expenses, make sure you do it sooner rather than later. Don't stall - it will only make the problems bigger later!

- After you tithe, pay yourself NEXT. Place the money in an account that is hard to get to so you won't be able to access it easily and spend it as freely. This is a great way to help you save money!

  Before you get married, be sure you can support yourself financially. This will give you great confidence later in life.
  – *Beth Darby Hurley from Faye Darby*

- When planning your budget, consider using envelopes for your different expenses (dry cleaning, clothes, groceries, weekend money, etc.). Place cash inside the envelopes and write on them each time you spend the money. This will help you see where your money is going and it will prevent you from overspending.

During special times, remember to take a few minutes to really soak up the moment.

- Watch *White Christmas* and *It's A Wonderful Life* every year.

- Start a Thankful Box at the beginning of the year. Cover a shoe box with wrapping paper and put a slit in the top. Write down each day or week at dinner time something you are thankful for. On Thanksgiving Day open the box and take turns reading the slips of paper. It's a great way to remember the things you are grateful for.

- To decorate a Christmas tree: First, wrap LOTS & LOTS of lights around the branches and deep within the branches. Second, add solid reflective balls DEEP into the base of the tree. This reflects the light and makes it seem as if there are twice as many lights. Finally, place ornaments on the outside branches. Place your favorite ones front and center. You can use floral wire to make ornaments hang higher or lower to fill in the tree's gaps and holes.

- At Christmas time, decorate the house first, then get the tree and bring in all the boxes with decorations in them. Otherwise you will have boxes everywhere! After Christmas, put all the house decorations away first and then take down the tree.

Ever since my husband and I started dating, we have exchanged Christmas ornaments. We met on the first day of college our freshman year and now we have been married for over twenty-four years. When the kids came along we included them in our little tradition. The ornaments are sometimes fancy, sometimes silly, and sometimes homemade. The only requirement is that they somehow mark an event that occurred during our year. It can be an accomplishment, reaching a goal, a particular struggle, anything relevant to that particular year in our lives. Every year as we put up our Christmas tree, it becomes an incredible time of retelling our family history. As each of us hangs an ornament, we tell its story. We laugh, cry, cheer and everything in between. It has become an incredible way to preserve our family history. The kids can even tell the various stories of how we came to be who we are.

– Maria Lutzel

- Store your Christmas decorations in wine boxes that have dividers in them. Another option is to use large Ziploc bags - blow air into them and then seal. This creates a bubble wrap effect and protects the ornaments from breaking.

- Keep your Christmas list somewhere in your phone or planner so throughout the year when you come across deals or sales you can see who you need to buy for and if any of the items will work for someone on the list.

- Go through your children's Halloween candy and divide it into groups by type of candy using sandwich/snack size Ziplocs. This keeps the candy from mixing with flavors that may affect the taste. This also allows you to get rid of any candy you don't want your children to have.

- Save the corks from special events and holidays that you share with special people in your life. You can use them later to make something special, like a cork board of memories.

- Make handprint tiles with your loved ones each year during the holidays. You can use them to make a special table, decorate a bathroom or simply place them in stands around the house. I started doing this when my children were infants and we still do it every year on their birthdays.

- Before the rush of the holidays, make and freeze casseroles for holiday dinners or to use for busy nights when you don't have the time or energy to prepare dinner. This will help cut down on the frenzy of the season and also allow more time to just be together.

- If your holiday schedule isn't working for you and you are frustrated then it's time for new traditions! Holidays should be enjoyed, not dreaded, so create a new "norm" that brings you happiness.

- This holiday season, take pictures of how you place your decorations, crafts you make, designs you like, etc. This will serve as a reference for next year, so you can remember how you made something or how you decorated the house.

You can make garland look extravagant by weaving real evergreen onto fake garland pieces. Hold the evergreen in place using the wire from the fake garland or use floral wire. This works best outdoors, but it can be used inside if you "mist" the evergreen frequently. *– Annette Smith*

Always read *The Night Before Christmas* on Christmas Eve, even if you don't have kids. It's a wonderful holiday tradition. *– Beth Darby Hurley*

Etiquette
& Manners

> You can say anything as long as you end it with "Bless her heart!"

- Don't be a snob. Unless of course they deserve it and then it becomes necessary.

- When you tell someone you are sorry, look them straight in the eye.

- Never laugh at anyone's dreams. People who don't have dreams don't have much.

- When you realize you have made a mistake, take immediate action to correct it.

- To get out of a car like a lady: keep your legs together, then turn on your bottom and get out of the car.

- When you have cold hands and you have to shake hands with someone say, "Cold hands but warm heart."

- When someone asks you a question that you really do not want to answer, look them in the eye, smile and ask, "Why do you want to know?" or "Why do you ask?"

- When you disagree with someone and they don't understand your point say, "That just does not work for ME."

- When handling a confrontation use the "sandwich" technique: say something positive and uplifting, address the issue, and then close with another positive. For example: "You know I love you and I respect your opinion. However, I disagree with you on this decision and I must let you know. I appreciate you and think you are wonderful."

- To fully understand what someone is trying to tell you, repeat back to them what they are asking you. Say, "Let me understand what you are saying," and repeat back to them what they said. If you don't appreciate what they are asking, return their question with a question.

- Learn how to "work a crowd" to make everyone feel welcome. Circulate, Dahhhling, Circulate!

- NEVER show up empty-handed.

- She who talks the most knows the least.

- Stay Classy! Be the kind of lady who not only impresses men, but also women.

- Mail HANDWRITTEN thank you notes. Don't just say "Thanks for the gift." Instead, give details about why you like the gift and how you will use it in the future.

- Keep a small pack of matches in your purse in case you use the restroom and need to clear the air afterwards.

- Be wary of people who don't look you in the eye when they speak to you. They could be lying, not interested or hiding something. YOU should look people in the eye when you are speaking to them or when they are talking to you.

- When you are at a fancy dinner with lots of silverware and you are not sure what to use, remember to work your way in towards the plate. The shorter fork is for your salad, etc.

- Leave before they want you to!

- Sometimes you just need to CLOSE your mouth. You can decrease your credibility by talking too much.

If you are out to dinner and can't remember which is your bread plate or drink, and not your neighbor's, make a little "b" and "d" with your fingers. The hand that makes the "b" is on the side of your bread plate and the hand that makes the "d" is on the side of your drink. - *Stephanny deGorter*

- If you are eating at someone's home and you don't care for what they prepared, take a "thank you" bite. It's not only the polite thing to do, but you may discover you like it!

- If someone is engaged, pregnant or has made a big sale you will find out about it. Don't ask them! If they aren't/haven't, you will make them feel bad. They will certainly tell you if they have good news they want to share!

- If someone says something to you that is inappropriate, rude, nosey or negative, simply change the subject right away and they will usually realize they have made a mistake.

- When someone has something happen to them that is sad just say, "I AM SO SORRY." People make the mistake of saying things such as "It was for the best," or "Things happen for a reason." Just simply say "I am sorry," or "I hurt for you," and leave it at that.

- Think before you speak. There is A LOT of power in the spoken word.

- Talk slowly, but think quickly and listen carefully.

About
the Author

Jo Ann Darby

Jo Ann Darby is a Certified Personal Trainer (AFAA), Licensed Medical Esthetician, and North Carolina Esthetics Educator. She has worked as a Fitness Consultant for the Teen Tone Extreme Workout Video (Four Crossings Entertainment), as well as a Featured Model in *Muscle Media Magazine.*

Jo Ann currently owns Lake Norman Skin Studio Medi-Spa in Cornelius, NC. She has been married to her husband, Allen, for 18 years, with whom she has a son, Trevor (13) and a daughter and "Girlfriend," Alana (11).